No. 56: YORK

The Transition Years – Steam to Diesel

Photographs by the late **KEITH R PIRT** *Compiled by* **ROGER HILL**

Copyright Book Law Publications 2010
ISBN 978-1-907094-60-6

INTRODUCTION

York has arguably more structures of outstanding architectural significance than any UK City outside London. There is little doubt that the Minster takes pride of place but in the writer's view the runner up is the magnificent trainshed opened by the North Eastern Railway in 1877. Its great curved roof is supported by five splendid arches, the largest of which is 48 feet high with a span of 81 feet. Electrification of the ECML between 1987 and 1989 involved major alterations to the station, including removal of the centre roads, and it is to the great credit of those responsible for the design that the finished article is far from being unsightly. Indeed it is possible to stand on the platform and be completely unaware of the catenary, so tastefully has the work been undertaken. This book however is not intended to be a history of York's railways, that and the activities of George Hudson, The Railway King, are well documented elsewhere. No, this is the railways of York and the surrounding area as viewed through the camera of the late Keith Pirt. Keith spent much time here and his first book "Real Steam in Colour-- York" was published in 1990. The writer has made strenuous efforts to find previously unseen material but no apology is either given or intended for including a small number of the pictures which first appeared in that early work, of which Keith was rightly intensely proud. So sit back, relax and enjoy a master photographer's Memories of York and Surrounding Area.

Roger Hill, Howden, November 2010

Cover Picture

Stanier LMS Princess Coronation pacific 46229 DUCHESS OF HAMILTON stands at platform 9 under the great arched roof of York station with a SCARBOROUGH SPA EXPRESS working in the summer of 1983. At that time the flagship of the NRM fleet, she was built as a streamliner at Crewe and put into traffic on 7 September 1938. The streamlined casing was removed in January 1948 and her BR career ended on 15 February 1964 when she was bought by Sir Billy Butlin for open air static display at his holiday camp at Minehead. With her condition rapidly deteriorating, she was thankfully taken into the care of the NRM in 1976 and who can forget that tear jerking day in 1980 when a Duchess hauled a passenger train for the first time in 16 years? Controversially she has now been re-streamlined and whilst she looks no less majestic in this condition, it is doubtful that she will ever steam again.............but never say never! Photo by Roger Hill

Title Page Picture

All but 25 of the 184 Gresley V2 2-6-2s were built at Darlington. As originally constructed, all three cylinders were in a single monobloc casting, but between May 1956 and February 1962, 71 engines were rebuilt with three separate cylinders. The rebuilds were instantly recognisable by their outside steampipes. Here, original monobloc 60974 leaves the station with an up express in May 1959, passing the NER South shed, the roofed building dating from 1851 and the roofless one from 1863. 60974 entered traffic from Darlington as LNER 3686 in August 1943 and was withdrawn in December 1963. *KRP E17*

Printed and bound by The Amadeus Press, Cleckheaton, West Yorkshire
First published in the United Kingdom by Book Law Publications, 382 Carlton Hill, Nottingham, NG4 1JA

With the Minster prominent in the background Peppercorn Class K1 2-6-0 62065 rounds Leeman Road curve hauling the York breakdown train on an unrecorded date. 62065 was built by North British, works number 26669, and put into traffic in January 1950. She was withdrawn in March 1967 and stored until being cut up at Drapers in August of that year. The 75 ton steam breakdown crane DB 967159 was delivered new to York from Cowans-Sheldon in 1962, one of a batch of twelve ordered in 1960 as part of the Modernisation Plan. Keith photographed this crane separately and apparently standing on the down main line at Leeman Road and recorded the date as June 1965. It is therefore reasonable to assume that both pictures were taken on the same day. Note the delightfully ancient coaches in the consist. *KRP NP453*

Double chimney BR Standard 9F 2-10-0 92231 simmers in York's Leeman Road shed yard (50A) in June 1966. She was one of a batch reallocated to York from Feltham on the Southern Region in September 1963, having previously been at Eastleigh for working the Fawley - Southampton - Toton oil trains. She was built at Crewe in August 1958 and was withdrawn just over **EIGHT YEARS** later in November 1966 and cut up by Drapers of Hull in April 1967. What a scandalous waste of resources. *KRP B148*

Ex-works BR Standard Class 3 2-6-0 77012 in the shed yard in June 1965, standing in front of a dirty, unidentified and nameplate-less Jubilee and alongside LMS Ivatt Class 4 2-6-0 43138. Turned out of Swindon in June 1954, 77012 was a North Eastern Region resident all her life, half of which was spent at 50A, where she was primarily employed hauling officers' inspection saloons. In this picture however, she is carrying a 55F Bradford Manningham shed-plate. Withdrawn in June 1967, she was the penultimate survivor of her class and was outlived only by the wandering 77014, which finished her days at Guildford on the Southern. *KRP B157*

Keith left no details of this shot of an unidentified Class 45 diesel heading a Newcastle - Liverpool express past the well known milepost at Beningbrough, north of York, probably in the late summer of 1981. *KRP 67137.1*

Deltic 55008 THE GREEN HOWARDS heads a York - Kings Cross "stopper" past Barlby on the ECML north of Selby in September 1981. This section of the main line was closed on the opening of the Selby Coalfield Diversion on 3 October 1983 and now forms part of the A19 trunk road. 55008's last duty was the 21.20 Aberdeen - Kings Cross on 29 December 1981 and only flat batteries prevented her from being employed on that hectic last day, 31 December. *KRP D95*

In August 1979 Class 45 diesel 45025 heads an up express past the sewage works opposite Skelton yard before passing under Clifton bridge and rounding Severus curve, north of Leeman Road yard and the National Railway Museum. *KRP D99*

A Kings Cross - York "stopper" is seen amongst the rosebay willowherb, looking south from the same viewpoint as picture D95 above, in July 1981. This Deltic is 55004 QUEEN'S OWN HIGHLANDER, which met her nemesis after failing at Liverpool three months later. *KRP D179*

In September 1981, a Bristol – Newcastle express hauled by Class 45 45043, then named THE KING'S OWN ROYAL BORDER REGIMENT, powers past the empty, soon-to-be-busy Gascoigne Wood Sidings, en route to Selby and York. In the intervening thirty or so years to date the adjoining Gascoigne Wood Colliery has opened, produced and closed so the sidings are once again empty. The original, impressive signal box (out of shot) survives as a reminder of more prosperous times. *KRP D185*

A down Newcastle express passes Beningbrough in September 1981 headed by 55008 THE GREEN HOWARDS which has featured elsewhere in this book. *KRP D191*

Keith has left no details whatsoever of this impressive study of unidentified Class 45 and Deltic diesels in the shed yard, with York Minster dominating the background. *KRP NP162*

An unidentified Class 31 diesel passes Dringhouses Marshalling Yard with an up express. Comparison of the position of the few wagons in the otherwise deserted yard with those in the picture on page 96 of Keith's Diesel Colour Portfolio book, dates it as September 1981. Dringhouses Yard was opened in 1961 as a hump marshalling yard, the first in the country specifically built to handle fully braked express freight. It closed in 1987 when air-braked Speedlink services were relocated to Doncaster and the site is now a (very large!) housing estate. *KRP NP182*

Yes it's been published before but this shot of Thompson A2/2 pacific 60501 COCK O' THE NORTH passing Leeman Road yard with a down Newcastle express in May 1959 deserves to be seen again. She came out of Doncaster rebuilt from Class P2 2-8-2 2001 in September 1944, was transferred to 50A in December 1950 and withdrawn from there in February 1960. Photographs exist of her, *COMPLETE WITH THOSE PRICELESS NAMEPLATES*, languishing, deserted, in Doncaster Works scrapyard! Note the neatly tended gardens, for many years a feature of this area of the yard. Note also the "whiskered" Birmingham RC&W DMU, unavoidably standing alongside, unavoidably since Keith would *NEVER* have permitted such an intrusion into one of his classic slides had he had a choice in the matter! *KRP E21*

Immaculate, lifelong Newcastle allocated, double chimney Gresley A3 pacific 60085 MANNA stands by the South shed in May 1959. Built at Doncaster as LNER 2596 in February 1930, MANNA was to have trough smoke deflectors fitted in April 1962, before meeting her doom at Drapers of Hull in December 1964. *KRP E25*

With the Royal Station Hotel as the backdrop, Thompson A2/3 pacific 60517 OCEAN SWELL curves out of the station with a down Newcastle express in May 1959. OCEAN SWELL was turned out from Doncaster in November 1946 and was cut up at her birthplace in April 1963. *KRP E39*

Billed at the time as the last A4 working out of Kings Cross, 60009 UNION OF SOUTH AFRICA hauled THE JUBILEE REQUIEM special to Newcastle and back on 24 October 1964. UNION did not disgrace the reputation of her class by arriving back at The Cross on the return trip 26 minutes early, having reached 96mph en route! Keith caught the northbound special passing the British Oil & Cake Mills at Selby. UNION's exploits in preservation are the stuff of legends. *KRP E126*

Original monobloc cylinder V2 60895 goes on York North shed in October 1964. She was built at Darlington, being turned out as LNER 4866 in January 1940, was allocated to 50A from 1953 and was withdrawn in April 1965. *KRP E127*

By contrast to 60895, also in the North shed yard in October 1964, is 60847 ST PETER'S SCHOOL, YORK, AD 627, rebuilt with three separate cylinders and outside steampipes and by then running *sans* nameplates. She was built at Darlington as LNER 4818 in March 1939 and for all but four months of her entire life was allocated to 50A, being withdrawn on 17 July 1965. She was named in the station by the School's head boy on 3 April 1939 and the nameplates bore the School's colours and badge. One of the plates was presented to the School one week after 60847 was withdrawn and at auction in 2010, the other realised no less than £24,000! *KRP E769*

In August 1959, one of the last remaining single chimney A3s 60069 SCEPTRE stands near 50A's massive reinforced concrete coaling plant. This awe inspiring edifice, built in 1932, was 100 feet high, had a coal capacity of 500 tons and could replenish two locomotives at a time. It was problematically demolished in 1970, only as a last resort with the aid of steel hawsers attached to locomotives! SCEPTRE was originally built as LNER Class A1 2568 by North British in September 1924, was rebuilt to an A3 at Doncaster in May 1942 and returned to Doncaster for cutting up in May 1963. Her double chimney was eventually fitted a month after this picture was taken and she never received the trough smoke deflectors. The LMS Fowler pattern tender behind almost certainly belongs to unrebuilt Patriot 4-6-0 45517, visiting from Bank Hall shed, Liverpool. *KRP E157*

A4 pacific 60026 MILES BEEVOR heads the up Scotch Goods past the allotments at Holgate Road platforms, south of the station, in October 1959. This freight was a Kings Cross Top Link working and so the appearance of an A4 on it was not unusual. 60026 was built as LNER 4485 KESTREL in February 1937 and renamed in November 1947. She was one of the lucky A4s which went out in a blaze of glory working the Glasgow - Aberdeen three hour expresses and was withdrawn from Aberdeen, Ferryhill in December 1965. Her remains were put to the torch at Hughes Bolckow's yard at North Blyth but not before she had donated some of her vital organs, in particular her coupled wheels, to the restored 4498 SIR NIGEL GRESLEY. *KRP E165*

Thompson Class B1 4-6-0 61024 ADDAX with a heavy southbound freight which has been routed through the station approaches Holgate Road bridge in August 1959. The freight avoiding lines run from and into Holgate Junction on the left. ADDAX was built at Darlington, works number 2064, and entered traffic in May 1947. She was withdrawn from Thornaby shed in May 1966. Note outside the station on the right a V2 and LMS Jinty 0-6-0T 47556, one of a handful of these locomotives allocated to 50A alongside the J72s for pilot duties. *KRP E188*

The writer well remembers his move to the York area in early 1959 and as an excited 14 year old, "copping" all the three cylinder NER Class S3, LNER B16 4-6-0s the vast majority of which always seemed to be allocated to 50A. Here is B16/3 61467 leaving the station with a Scarborough - Leeds train in June 1959. She was one of 17 of the class rebuilt by Thompson between 1944 and 1949 with three separate sets of Walschaerts valve gear. Entering traffic from Darlington in December 1923 as LNER 1383; 61467 was cut up by Drapers in October 1964. *KRP E191*

Original Raven NER B16/1 61416 propels a rake of brake vans under Holgate Road bridge in May 1959. Built at Darlington as NER 920 in September 1920, she was allocated to 50A virtually continuously from 1936 until withdrawal and cutting up at Darlington North Road in May 1961. Holgate Road bridge, which exists in substantially the same condition today, was opened in 1911 having been widened to accommodate trams. In 1989 it was altered again, this time raised to permit the installation of the overhead electric catenary. *KRP E202*

Thompson A2/3 pacific 60511 AIRBORNE passes Dringhouses Yard with a Newcastle - Kings Cross express in October 1959. Allocated to the Newcastle area for virtually all her life, AIRBORNE entered traffic from Doncaster in July 1946 and was withdrawn in November 1962. Note that she is carrying the lipped chimney, in the writer's opinion far more pleasing on the eye than the sheet metal slab type fitted to some other members of the class and incidentally, also currently to the new A1 60163 TORNADO. *KRP E211*

Keith notes that in August 1959, ex Doncaster Works Gresley Class K3 2-6-0 61927 was specially posed for him with rods down between the York shed coaler and the 70 foot turntable! Built by Armstrong Whitworth as LNER 2936, 61927 entered traffic on 1 January 1935 and was cut up at Doncaster in July 1961, during the great K3 cull of 1961/62. *KRP E212*

The history of Peppercorn K1 62005 during her 43 years of preservation is well known, but here is the celebrity in York shed yard ex Darlington Works in May 1965. Built by North British, works number 26609, in June 1949, she was the last Eastern Region locomotive in BR service when withdrawn from Leeds Holbeck shed on 30 December 1967. *KRP E290*

This has been published before but colour pictures (especially of this quality) of North Eastern Class R, LNER D20, 4-4-0s are not exactly plentiful so the writer claims compiler's licence! On 23 June 1957 the RCTS ran THE YORKSHIRE COAST RAILTOUR from Leeds to Whitby via York, a trip on the Easingwold Railway (see picture E913) and on to Scarborough via Gilling and Bridlington to Whitby, returning to York over the present North Yorkshire Moors Railway. D20 62387 was specially brought down from Alnmouth for this train and worked from Leeds as far as York Holgate Road, believed to have been be the last occasion this station was used by a passenger train. The station was opened in about 1860 and used principally for race traffic until closed in 1939. However, the platforms remained in situ and in good condition until they were removed in 1964 and many readers will recall their well maintained gardens with "YORK" picked out in flowers. *KRP E362*

Later on 23 June 1957 the RCTS Railtour visited the Easingwold Railway, an impecunious Col. Stephens-like undertaking, which operated over the two and a half miles between Alne on the ECML and Easingwold, where Keith took this picture. This Light Railway had escaped nationalisation in 1948 and managed to stagger on independently until complete closure later in 1957. NER Class J71 0-6-0T 68246, built in 1889 and withdrawn in November 1958, officiated. She was hired from BR, having been nominally allocated to 50A since time immemorial. The faithful were conveyed standing in open wagons and in an LNER six wheel passenger brake van. Just a couple of rickety ladders and not a hard hat nor a high vis jacket in sight! Health and safety? What's that? *KRP E913*

March, Cambs, allocated K3 61929 hauls a heavy freight through the station and towards Holgate Road in May 1959. Built by Robert Stephensons as LNER 1325 in 1934, she was cut up at Doncaster in May 1962. *KRP E396*

Perhaps the most bizarre of all post BR nationalisation locomotive construction was the order for 28 more Class J72 0-6-0Ts built in 1949-51 to the original 1898 NER design. In May 1959 the York station south end pilot is 69016 of this batch, turned into traffic from Darlington (works number 2097) on 9 January 1950 and withdrawn just fourteen years later in October 1964. *KRP E412*

Gateshead's double chimney, not TOO dirty, A3 60078 NIGHT HAWK draws to a halt at platform 8 south with a Newcastle - Kings Cross express in August 1959. Built by North British as A1 LNER 2577 in 1924, NIGHT HAWK was rebuilt to an A3 in January 1944, would receive trough deflectors in March 1962 and was cut up at Doncaster in May 1963. Note the double yellow signal for platform 9, probably for a down express. *KRP E473*

Coming off the freight avoiding line at Holgate Junction, past the South shed, in May 1959 is an up goods behind clean, Mexborough allocated B1 61112. She was released to traffic by North British, works number 25868, on 27 December 1946 and sold for scrap exactly sixteen years later. *KRP E539*

Keith described this portrait of Peppercorn Class A1 pacific 60124 KENILWORTH in York North yard, in October 1964 as "superb", and he was not wrong! At various times between 1958 and 1965, roughly a dozen A1s and several A2s were allocated to 50A. The writer, as a schoolboy "number cruncher" of the time, recalls often being surprised at the large number of them to be found on and around the shed or in the workshop.....anywhere in fact except out on the main line. Keith's pictures tell a similar story for he has many 50A A1s in the yard and the roundhouse but very few actually working trains. The reason for this from about 1961 was of course the coming of the Class 40s, 47s and 55s. KENILWORTH was built at Doncaster (works number 2041) and released to traffic in March 1949. She was scrapped at Drapers in May 1966, survived only by 60145 SAINT MUNGO. *KRP E554*

Another of the ubiquitous NER B16s, original part 1 engine 61456 brings a southbound freight off the avoiding line at Holgate Junction in May 1959. She was built as LNER 1373 in October 1924 and scrapped at Darlington North Road in August 1960. *KRP E659*

With just a month of life left, monobloc cylinder V2 60963 stands in the yard in May 1965. Turned out of Darlington as LNER 3675 in January 1943, in October 1959 she became the first of the handful of the class to be fitted with a double chimney in an effort to improve steaming. The type of arrangement selected for her however was not the most effective, being similar to that on the LMS Royal Scots, rather than the Kylchap blastpipe as fitted to the Eastern Region pacifics. There was little or no improvement in her poor steaming, resulting in her withdrawal from 50A in June 1965, (where she had been continuously allocated since 1948) as the last surviving double chimney V2. *KRP E700*

Another lifelong York monobloc V2, 60968, storms round Leeman Road curve past the full loco yard with a rake of mainly Gresley coaches forming a down express in October 1959. As LNER 3680 she came from Darlington in April 1943 and was cut up at Doncaster in May 1963. *KRP E747*

York North goods yard was a location not often photographed by Keith and here is K1 62057 leaving with an up freight in October 1964. Built by North British in November 1949 with works number 26661, 62057 was transferred away from 50A to North Blyth in March 1966, was withdrawn on 1 May 1967 and scrapped at Arnott Young's yard at Dinsdale in July 1967. *KRP E798*

Hardly looking like the world's most famous steam locomotive, 60103 FLYING SCOTSMAN arrives in Leeman Road sidings with an up parcels in August 1959. 4472 was put into traffic at Doncaster as an A1 in February 1923 and returned to traffic rebuilt as an A3 on 4 January 1947. A double chimney was fitted in January 1959 and trough deflectors in December 1961. Withdrawal from BR service and immortality came on 14 January 1963.......the rest as they say is history! The enormous debt of gratitude owed by all to Alan Pegler is surely no less today than nearly half a century ago. *KRP E851*

Keith's favourite location at Holgate Junction with the last V2 to be built, Kings Cross Top Shed's monobloc 60983 taking the heavily loaded up SCARBOROUGH FLYER out of the station in August 1959. LNER 3695 was turned out of Darlington in July 1944 and was allocated to 34A from October 1946 until withdrawal in June 1962 when she was scrapped at Doncaster. Despite being a regular 34A V2 or even an A4 working, THE SCARBOROUGH FLYER lasted little longer than 60983, disappearing from the schedules at the end of the 1962 summer timetable. *KRP E860*

Leeman Road yard in October 1964 finds local A1 60140 BALMORAL, waiting for work which isn't there, coupled to Gateshead's May 1960-delivered, English Electric Class 40 diesel D273. BALMORAL was put into traffic by Darlington on Christmas Eve 1948 and was a 50A resident for her whole life save for eight months at Kings Cross in 1949/50. She met her end at Drapers in April 1965, one of ten A1s despatched at that yard. *KRP E862*

A special bound for Scarborough leaves platform 15 or 16 and makes for Waterworks Crossing (see the last picture in this book) and the bridge over the River Ouse behind local B1 61031 REEDBUCK in May 1964. This B1 was out-shopped from Darlington in July 1947 and scrapped at Drapers in November 1964. *KRP E951*

Another pair of lightly worked big LNER locos in the shed yard in October 1964. Separate cylinder and outside steampipe fitted V2 60929 is with A1 60124 KENILWORTH, which has already featured in this book. 60929 was one of the minority of the class to be built at Doncaster, from where she was put into traffic in June 1941 as LNER 3656. She was rebuilt with three separate cylinders in 1960 and was cut up by Cashmores in August 1965. *KRP E1079*

A panoramic view of the south end of York station in May 1959. Double chimney A3 60109 HERMIT stands in platform 9 on an up Kings Cross express, in the centre is V2 60974 (featured elsewhere in this book) and on the far right a B1 is in platform 3. HERMIT was one of the first batch of Gresley A1 pacifics; built at Doncaster and turned out as LNER 4478 in July 1923. She was rebuilt to an A3 in November 1943, acquired her double chimney in March 1959 and would be fitted with trough deflectors in January 1961. For many years a favoured Top Shed A3 and usually kept in immaculate condition, HERMIT was cut up at her birthplace in December 1962. *KRP E1109*

Looking very smart in her clean black livery, south end pilot NER J72 0-6-0T 68677 stands in the sun under Holgate Road bridge in August 1959. She was built at Darlington as NER 1746 in 1898 and spent all but one of her 63 years at York, being scrapped in December 1961. Note the cattle wagons on the left and the express passenger headlamps which were carried by all the York station pilots. *KRP E1198*

It is not known which, if any, of this trio of B16/1s in open storage outside the South shed in May 1959 was ever steamed again, although 61428 may have been since she received a casual / light repair at Darlington in September 1959. From left to right they are 61471 (LNER 842 of December 1919, cut up at North Road in September 1960); 61428 (LNER 933 of March 1921, cut at North Road November 1960) and 61431 (LNER 937 of May 1921, also scrapped at North Road, in November 1961). 61471 was formerly numbered BR 61402 but in 1949, in common with the rest of the 61400 - 09 series had to be renumbered from 61469 to 61478 to make way for new B1s. *KRP E1201*

Immaculate double chimney A3 60105 VICTOR WILD arrives at York under Holgate Road bridge with a down Kings Cross - Tyne Commission Quay Boat Express in May 1959. Sailings to Norway departed from this Quay where the railway ran right up to the side of the ship. These services operated until 1970 by which time it was accepted that air travel was here to stay. VICTOR WILD was one of the original batch of twelve A1s, emerging from Doncaster in March 1923. She was rebuilt as an A3 in October 1942, acquired her double chimney in March 1959 and would be fitted with trough deflectors in December 1960. She was reduced to a pile of scrap at Doncaster in August 1963. Note the Great Northern pattern railed tender which was common to all the 60102 - 12 batch save for FLYING SCOTSMAN and 60111 ENTERPRISE. *KRP E1205*

A glimpse inside the roundhouse in May 1967. FLYING SCOTSMAN has arrived on THE CATHEDRALS EXPRESS special from Norwich and is being cleaned by Mr George Hinchcliffe and his team. Also on show is preserved A4 60019 BITTERN which was kept at York from her purchase by the late Mr Geoff Drury in September 1966 until 1971 when she was moved to Leeds Neville Hill, there to find herself in the company of K1 62005, Gresley K4 2-6-0 3442 THE GREAT MARQUESS and GER N7 0-6-2T 69621. Under the eagle eye of the York shedmaster the late Mr Geoff Bird, the writer was one of the small team which worked on the restoration of BITTERN in those early days. The work parties were known to go on until (very) late and the writer well remembers Mr Bird pleading with the team to leave so that he could go home to bed! He could of course simply have thrown us out but Mr Bird would never do anything so crude, he was a gentleman of the first order! *KRP E1210*

Viewed from the permanent way yard on the outside of Severus (otherwise known as Clifton) curve, north of Leeman Road in May 1959, rebuilt V2 60932 of Newcastle Heaton shed heads an up freight. Built at Doncaster and turned out as LNER 3659 in October 1941, she was one of a batch despatched to Swindon Works for scrapping in August 1964. *KRP E1212*

It is the lighting which makes this an outstanding picture of two more apparently unemployed York A1s in the shed yard in October 1964. Virtually a lifelong resident is 60146 PEREGRINE, a Darlington product (works number 2065) of April 1949, whereas 60155 BORDERER came from Doncaster (works number 2049) five months later. Both were scrapped by Wards at Killamarsh near Rotherham in November 1965. BORDERER was one of a batch of five of the class fitted with Timken roller bearings on all axles, a modification which resulted in considerably higher mileages being achieved between major repairs. *KRP E1376*

Inside the roundhouse, now the Great Hall of the NRM, in May 1965. Five locomotives are on view, a shining, rebuilt V2 60831, two LMS Ivatt Class 4 2-6-0s, 43097 with a second one unidentified and two WD 2-8-0s, 90217 and another unidentified. The V2 came from Darlington in May 1938 as LNER 4802 and was rebuilt with separate cylinders and outside steampipes in May 1957. In February 1967 she became one of surprisingly only two V2s to be scrapped by Drapers in Hull, 60961 (another York resident) being the other. 60831 was the last surviving English V2 and the penultimate survivor of the whole class, being outlived by only four weeks by 60836 at Dundee. 43097 was built at Darlington in January 1951 and withdrawn in July 1967; 90217 came from North British as WD 77260 in November 1943 and was withdrawn in October 1965. *KRP E1402*

A touch of art by Keith in the yard in April 1965......the front ends of Stanier LMS 8F 2-8-0 48373 and two K1s, on the right 62005 and behind, another unidentified. The celebrated 62005 is featured elsewhere in this book. The 8F, ex Darlington Works and presumably en route back to her home at Stockport Edgeley came from Horwich in November 1944 and survived almost to the end of steam, until June 1968. *KRP E1434*

Double chimney A3 60056 CENTENARY brings a down express round Leeman Road curve in September 1959. Constructed at Doncaster as A1 2555 in February 1925, rebuilt to an A3 in August 1944, the double chimney and (later) trough deflectors were added respectively in July 1959 and July 1961. She was cut up at her birthplace in May 1963, having been allocated to Grantham for ten years prior to her demise. *KRP E1446*

On a cold day in January 1967, England's last surviving V2 60831 (compare her condition with that in picture E1402!) is awaiting her final journey to Hull and oblivion. The writer's own records of the period show that the 9F seen behind 60831 was 92060 or possibly 92097 (Crewe 1955 and 1956 respectively), two of the celebrated Tyne Dock - Consett ore engines, both of which were stopped off at 50A en route to Drapers where they were cut up on 10 April 1967. York shed closed to regular steam in June 1967 and its last five engines, four B1s plus 77012 (previously featured in this book) were transferred away, leaving the preserved A4 BITTERN as the only serviceable steam locomotive on the premises. *KRP E1457*

It is a sobering thought that FLYING SCOTSMAN has at the time of writing spent no less than 47 of her 87 years in preservation......but it had only been 16 months when Keith took this fine picture. 4472 is seen accelerating past Leeman Road heading the Gresley Society's **LONDON NORTH EASTERN FLIER** (note the difference in the spelling of "Flier" from that in The Scarborough "Flyer"!) in May 1964. Note also the LNER-style headboard and particularly the complete rake of maroon Gresley coaches. If only THAT were still available today......but there, some people will never be satisfied! *KRP E1493*

A skilfully composed back shot in Leeman Road yard in October 1964 with B1s 61087 and 61012 PUKU, sandwiching an unidentified WD 2-8-0. Allocated to 36A Doncaster from 1949, 61087 was a North British product of October 1946, works number 25843, and scrapped in Garnham's yard in Chesterfield in December 1965. PUKU was built at Darlington in November 1946 and from 1960 was allocated to 53A Hull Dairycoates. She was to move to York in December 1966 and be scrapped by Hughes Bolckow in August 1967. *KRP E1494*

Another rear shot, this time from June 1965 and with York Minster as a backdrop, of NER J27 0-6-0 65846 nose to nose with an unidentified B1 and a BR Standard tender, possibly a 9F, on the right. The J27, LNER 1213, was built by Beyer Peacock in 1908 and was withdrawn in October 1965. The B1 looks to have been prepared for the scrapyard before then. *KRP E1570*

Once again with the Minster dominating the background and once again standing unemployed in the shed yard in April 1965 are these two A1s, 60138 BOSWELL and 60155 BORDERER. BOSWELL was built at Darlington in December 1948 and, having been at 50A all her life, was reduced to scrap in Rotherham in November 1965. Her nameplates had been removed "for safe keeping" at least two months prior to that. BORDERER has already featured in this book. *KRP E1578*

In August 1959 one of the last remaining single chimney A3s 60069 SCEPTRE (which has already featured in this book) stands with some parcels vans at the south end of the station. She was just a month away from acquiring her Kylchap and indeed may even have actually been on her way to Doncaster to have it fitted since the records show that she was in works for a non-classified repair from 24 August until 4 September 1959. To avoid having to send a locomotive to works for this to be done, some of the larger sheds such as Kings Cross fitted the double chimneys "in house" but evidently Tweedmouth, where SCEPTRE was allocated at the time, did not have the necessary facilities. Note the shining Cravens DMU standing in the bay platform 10. *KRP E1621*

An up Newcastle - Kings Cross express passes Leeman Road behind Top Shed's A4 60013 DOMINION OF NEW ZEALAND in September 1959. Built in 1937 as LNER 4492, the last of the five "Dominion" A4s and painted garter blue for working the pre war CORONATION streamliner, 60013 was withdrawn in April 1963 and was not one of the lucky ones to escape to Scotland. Note the whistle presented by the New Zealand Government Railways which had a five tone, lower pitch but less musical note than normal A4 whistles. In September 1967 the writer took a haunting tape recording of this whistle fitted to SIR NIGEL GRESLEY and echoing off Wild Boar Fell at Ais Gill Summit. *KRP E1631*

Other than a couple of shots of FLYING SCOTSMAN from the 1960s it was not intended to include any preservation era pictures in this selection. However on looking through Keith's collection carefully, it became clear that strangely he has very little material in York station itself and nothing whatsoever under the great roof. The opportunity to redress the balance has been taken by including the picture on the cover of this book and by this historic shot of 4468 MALLARD standing at the south end of platform 9 in July 1988. There is the bonus of a Class 47 hauled up freight on the long removed centre road. Despite the obviously atrocious weather, Keith's masterful photographic skills shine through. *KRP P278*

Stanier LMS Jubilee 4-6-0 45717 DAUNTLESS comes on York shed after bringing in a Liverpool Exchange - Newcastle train in October 1959. These services ran via Rochdale and the Calder Valley line and were the preserve of 27A Liverpool Bank Hall shed. DAUNTLESS and her sisters MARS and GLORIOUS, as well as unrebuilt and unnamed Patriot 45517 were regular performers. 45717 was built at Crewe in July 1936 and scrapped at Cowlairs Works in February 1964. Strangely Keith does not appear to have turned his camera on the apparently ex-works V2 in the background, the nearest that can be found in his collection is Heaton's 60922 but his picture of that engine is dated August 1959.....we shall never know. One wonders what today's health and safety people would say about a railwayman hitching a ride in this unorthodox fashion? In those days nobody thought anything of it! *KRP M17*

Keith told the writer a tale about this fine picture taken at the south end of the station in August 1959. He was set up to fire his shutter as LMS Crab 2-6-0 42901 drew level with the pilot 69016 when without warning, this grimy monobloc V2 with a flared GC pattern tender appeared between the two. Fortunately his reactions were quick enough to capture this memorable result. The Crab, which was built at Crewe in August 1930 and withdrawn from Manchester Agecroft exactly 35 years later, was hauling a Scarborough - Leeds and Bradford holiday extra comprised of LMS stock. 69016 is featured elsewhere in this book. In the confusion Keith omitted to note the number of the V2! *KRP M104*

Heaton Mersey allocated 8F 2-8-0 48421 is ex Darlington Works in Leeman Road yard in October 1965, alongside B1 61158, visiting from Doncaster. The 8F was built at Swindon in December 1943 and taken into LMS stock in December 1949. She lasted until the end of steam in July 1968. The B1 was a Vulcan Foundry product of May 1947 and was withdrawn exactly 19 years later. *KRP M512*

In December 1934, North British delivered Jubilee 45589 GWALIOR which settled down to spend many years at Leeds Holbeck shed, being withdrawn from there in March 1965, although not cut up until a year later. She is seen here in September 1964 rounding the curve off Selby swing bridge with a down holiday excursion bound for Bridlington via the line to Market Weighton, up Enthorpe Bank to Driffield, thus avoiding congestion at Hull. 1964 was the last summer this useful double track line was to be available for it became a victim of the Beeching axe and closed completely on 14 June 1965. *KRP M515*

Midland three cylinder Compound 4-4-0 1000 stands in platform 8 south at York station in September 1959 with special reporting number M985, bound for Derby, as in the background an up express behind a V2 arrives in platform 9. The writer believes the Compound last to have been steamed in September 1983, since when she has been on static display in the NRM. *KRP M567*

A magnificently atmospheric shot inside the roundhouse in October 1964. From left to right are, B1 61018 GNU (the shortest name of any BR steam locomotive, HLI (as an acronym) doesn't count!, A1 pacific 60146 PEREGRINE (featured elsewhere in this book); another local B1, 61276 and the celebrated, now preserved NER Class P3 (LNER J27) 0-6-0 65894. GNU was out-shopped from Darlington in February 1947 and reduced to scrap at Drapers in December 1965 and 61276 was North British works number 26177 of January 1948 and cut up in August 1965. 65894, as NER 2392, was built at Darlington in September 1923 and withdrawn into the loving care of The North Eastern Locomotive Preservation Group (NELPG) in September 1967. *KRP NP32*

Until the advent of TORNADO in 2009, the last ECML passenger train to be hauled by a Peppercorn A1 was the 18.30 relief from York to Newcastle on 31 December 1965. The locomotive (which later returned to York with the empty stock) was 60145 SAINT MUNGO. She had been built at Darlington in March 1949, first withdrawn on 27 March 1966 but reinstated to 50A three weeks later and again withdrawn, this time to be to be cut up at Drapers in August 1966. Here is 60145 in the repair shop at York shed in either October 1964 or April 1965 (Keith does not give a date in this case), in the company of monobloc V2 60810 and another A1, possibly lifetime 50A resident 60121 SILURIAN. The V2 came from Darlington as LNER 4781 in September 1937 and met her end at Wath upon Dearne in January 1966. 60121 was also a Darlington product, of December 1948 and was cut by Wards of Killamarsh in November 1965. *KRP NP40*

In June 1922 Armstrong Whitworth put into traffic NER 2329, BR 68736, a J72 0-6-0T which in December 1958 was transferred from Harrogate Starbeck to York for station and carriage pilot duties. In spring 1960 the BR Publicity Department had the brilliant idea of repainting this engine together with sister 68723 at Newcastle in NER green, incorporating both the NER and BR crests. Here is 68736 in this livery in the station in June 1960, note again the express passenger headlamps. She was transferred in July 1961 to join 68723 at Newcastle and eventually outlived her sister, being scrapped at Darlington North Road in November 1963. The green livery has been perpetuated on the preserved J72 69023 JOEM. Note the failure to clean the tops of the dome and the boiler. *KRP NP354*

Single chimney A3 60061 PRETTY POLLY leaves York past Holgate Road platforms with an up express comprising mainly "blood and custard" stock, more of which appears in a down train on the left. PRETTY POLLY was built at Doncaster as LNER A1 2560 in July 1925 and rebuilt as an A3 in May 1944. A double chimney with (in this case) small wing smoke deflectors was to be fitted in October 1958 and these deflectors were to be replaced by troughs in February 1962. She was cut up at Doncaster in September 1963. Keith's failure to provide details of the date of this picture has necessitated some detective work on the part of the writer. The neat station gardens and full leaf on the trees say it was summer, the single chimney rules out 1959 and 60061 appears to be carrying a 35B Grantham shed plate. She was allocated to Grantham from October 1954 until February 1959 and 35B was recoded 34F in April 1958, ruling out the summer of 1958. Keith's earliest English (as opposed to his Irish) slides appear to date from around September/October 1956, meaning it is unlikely to have been in 1955 or 1956. Putting all these factors together it is the writer's considered opinion that this picture was taken in the summer of 1957, He hopes readers will (pardon the pun) follow his train of logic!! Any comments to the Publisher please! *KRP NP428*

Another slightly mysterious and previously unpublished picture shows A4 60019 BITTERN coming under Holgate Road bridge past the gardens with an up express of "blood and custard" stock. BITTERN was put into traffic from Doncaster as LNER 4464 in December 1937 and until reallocated to Scotland (where she spent the rest of her BR career) in October 1963, she was a Newcastle engine, albeit rather a clean one by Gateshead's usual standards! Preservation of course followed. In this picture she still has a single chimney, this is the only KRP slide of an A4 in this condition which the writer has been able to discover. The records show that she underwent a general repair at Doncaster between 31 July and 6 September 1957, emerging with a double chimney. It is therefore impossible for this picture to have been taken after 31 July 1957. Given these details and the information gleaned from the picture of PRETTY POLLY opposite, it seems likely that both pictures were taken on the same day, between say mid-May and the end of July 1957. Anyone disagree? *KRP NP430*

Haymarket's A4 60027 MERLIN rounds the north curve on the approach to York station with an up express on an unrecorded date. The crossing, which gave access to the Scarborough line from platforms 9 and 12 to 16, as well as from Branches goods yard to the west, was known as Waterworks Crossing and was named from the pump house visible here, which extracted water for the railway direct from the River Ouse. The crossing was taken out in April 1974. MERLIN was put into traffic as LNER 4486 in March 1937 and was Scottish property all her life, her first 25 years being spent at 64B. She was withdrawn in September 1965 and cut up two months later. She is carrying a reversed headboard, probably THE ELIZABETHAN which in 1960 she worked on no fewer than 74 occasions, 46 of them consecutively, not bad for an engine then already 23 years old! Headboards were commonly reversed on an engine's lamp bracket when not in use as they got in the way on the footplate or (in the case of an A4) blocked the tender corridor. The reversed headboard and the Gresley stock, which was unusual on the non-stop by then, suggest it was a Sunday when the named train did not run and the regular stock was out of use, possibly being cleaned and serviced. It is therefore the writer's considered opinion that this picture was taken on a Sunday and probably in the summer of 1960. *KRP PIRT217*